PAUL COOKSON is a poet and football fan who spends most of his time visiting schools to perform his poems while trying to find out any up-to-date information about Everton. As well as writing poems about football he plays five-a-side football . . . but not at the same time. Paul lives with Sally, Sam and Daisy in Retford, Nottinghamshire. Even though this is in the north Nottinghamshire/south Yorkshire area, for some reason Sam has decided to support West Ham United. Good for him.

One of Paul's ambitions is to write the words to a song that the crowd will sing at the match, either for Everton or England, or possibly both.

DAVID PARKINS is pants at football. He always was. He didn't like games at school: it was too cold and too muddy, and his legs looked like pale, knobbly twigs dangling out of his shorts. He used to skive off by drawing posters for the games teacher, and that's why he is now an illustrator and not David Beckham. He doesn't mind this. At least illustrators get to wear long trousers to hide their spindly legs.

GiVE uS A GOAL!

FOOtBALL POEMS BY
Paul Cookson

iLLuStRAteD BY
David Parkins

MACMILLAN CHILDREN'S BOOKS

Dedicated to all the friends I've ever played regular football with. Walmer Bridge Rec, Tarleton High School Football Team, Elizabethan High School Staff, The Potato 5, The Sunday Night 40+ five-a-side team

First published 2004 by Macmillan Children's Books
a division of Macmillan Publishers Limited
20 New Wharf Road, London N1 9RR
Basingstoke and Oxford
Associated companies throughout the world
www.panmacmillan.com

ISBN 978-0-330-43654-0

7 9 8 6

A CIP catalogue record for this book is available from the British Library.

Printed and bound in the UK by CPI Mackays, Chatham ME5 8TD

NIL SATIS NISI OPTIMUM

We'll beat you, defeat you, we're ready to roll
Stop your fancy fooling round and give us a goal!

We'll chase you, then race you, you can't catch a cold
Get the ball into the net and give us a goal!

We'll skin you and we'll win you cos we're back in control
More, more, shoot, score, give us a goal!

Stop your fancy footwork now and give us a goal!

Noddy Holder / Jim Lea
SLADE, 1978

CONTENTS

iNTRODUCTiON

Well, it's a book of two halves and I'm over the moon about it to be honest. The idea was to follow the fortunes of a football team throughout a season and write poems about the ups, downs, highs, lows etc. of being a supporter. I've always supported Everton – nearly forty years now. I love going to the matches whenever I can. I wanted to capture some of the atmosphere of those games. Plus I realized that the vast majority of football fans don't get to every single match, so their experiences needed to be reflected – watching on the telly, listening to the radio, teletext etc. The 2002–2003 season was a pretty good one to be following Everton, what with the first full season under David Moyes and the introduction of a certain young man – Wayne Rooney.

Obviously, as a collection aimed primarily at children, many of the poems are seen through the eyes of a youngster. Many of them are based on real experiences at real matches and there is an appendix at the back of the book for those interested in such statistics.

At the end of the day we had too many poems to fill one volume and so some had to be relegated to the subs bench and then eventually dropped. Nevertheless, here's the first team. I hope you enjoy reading them as much as I did writing them and whoever your team is, good luck to you.

Meanwhile, it's nearly three and time to kick off so here we go (here we go, here we go) . . .

Paul Cookson
JANUARY 2004

PS Special mentions to Gareth Owen and Roger McGough, fellow Evertonians, fellow poets. Good fellows indeed.

1

FiRSt HALF

POEM FOR THE FIRST DAY OF THE FOOTBALL SEASON

Brand-new start,
last season is history and meaningless

My team has no points
and neither has yours.

All things are possible
and all glory dreamable.

Everything is winnable.
Potential is unmissable.

The peak of faith is scaleable.
The mountain of hope is touchable.
The summit of belief, believable.

Ten to three on that first Saturday
and nothing dulls the taste.

Excitement and anticipation,
tangible and tasteable.

Unparalleled success attainable.
This could be the best season of our lives.

OF COURSE, I COULD BE WRONG

Warm up matches have all gone well
The strikers are on song
Lost of goals, it's looking good
This year could be the best for years
Of course . . . I could be wrong.

New players passing, gelling well
A sense they all belong
It bodes well for the future
This year could be the best for years
Of course . . . I could be wrong.

Fresh purpose and fresh vigour
To carry us along
They seem to be attacking more
This year could be the best for years
Of course . . . I could be wrong.

Young stars are on the verge
Confidence is strong
Everybody's positive
This year could be the best for years
Of course . . . I could be wrong.

Happy days could soon be here
The wait's been far too long
It's best not to count chickens
This year could be the best for years
Of course . . . I could be wrong.

Again

Success could be a word that rolls
Off everybody's tongue
This could be a new era
This year could be the best for years
Let's prove the others wrong.

HE JUST CAN'T KICK IT WITH HIS FOOT

John Luke from our team
Is a goal-scoring machine
Phenomenally mesmerizing but . . .
The sport is called football
But his boots don't play at all
Cos he just can't kick it with his foot.

He can skim it from his shin
He can spin it on his chin
He can nod it in the net with his nut
He can blow it with his lips
Or skip it off his hips
But he just can't kick it with his foot

With simplicity and ease
He can use his knobbly knees
To blast it past the keeper, both eyes shut
He can whip and flick it
Up with his tongue and lick it
But he still can't kick it with his foot

Overshadowing the best
With the power from his chest
Like a rocket from a socket he can put
The ball into the sack
With a scorcher from his back
But he just can't kick it with his foot

Baffling belief
With the ball between his teeth
He can dribble his way out of any rut
Hypnotize it with his eyes
Keep it up on both his thighs
But he just can't kick it with his foot

From his shoulder to his nose
He can juggle it and pose
With precision and incision he can cut
Defences straight in half
With a volley from his calf
But he just can't kick it with his foot

He can keep it off the deck
Bounce the ball upon his neck
With his ball control you should see him strut
He can flap it with both ears
To loud applause and cheers
But he just can't kick it with his foot

He can trap it with his tum
Direct it with his bum
Deflect it just by wobbling his gut
When he's feeling silly
He can even use his . . . ankle
But he just can't kick it with his foot.

FLUMP!

BOBBLE!

tHE CHOOSiNG

It's in the lap of the gods
Exactly who you are drawn to
The magical moment that decides
Whether you're red, white or blue
You don't choose the football team . . .
the football team chooses you

The highs, the lows, the thick and the thin,
Allegiance will always shine through
United you stand together forever
The heart forever is true
You don't choose the football team . . .
The football team chooses you

You are special, you are selected,
One of the chosen few
A bond that cannot be broken
There's nothing at all you can do
You don't choose the football team . . .
The football team chooses you

Sonnet to the team i love

Shall I compare thee to a Saturday
Three o'clock the start in the afternoon
For then I watch my champions at play
Praying that we taste the victory soon
My heart beats wildly in my youthful breast
As we strive forward, onwards, evermore
Attack with vigour, vim and youthful zest
Perchance to shoot, perchance to even score
I swear allegiance to my belov'd team
Though days be dark and bleak as is the night
Perchance to wish, perchance to even dream
Of glories now within our mortal sight
     So long as men can breathe or eyes can see
     We will support the cause and follow thee.

PETRARCHAN SONNET FOR THE TEAM I LIKE LEAST

With vengeance and with passion it is true
That there's a football team I love to hate
Whose skills and style I can't appreciate
Because they play in red shirts, not in blue
It's not just me, for thousands feel it too
Although their players may be good or great
It's natural for them to irritate
With arrogance and pride in all they do.

I wish upon them losses and defeats
Though there be no logic to my reason
I pray they're thrashed and humiliated
Discontentment ever be their season
May their smug fans be squirming in their seats
Last not least, may they get relegated.

tHE FOOtBALLER'S PRAYER

Our team
Which art eleven
Hallowed be thy game
Our match be won
Their score be none
On turf as we score at least seven
Give us today no daily red . . . card
And forgive us our lost passes
As we forgive those who lose passes against us
Lead us not into retaliation
And deliver us from all fouls
For three is the kick off
The power and scorer
For ever and ever
Full time

PRE-MATCH RITUALS

Going to the match with Dad,
there's always the rituals.
Every home game, rain or shine –
The same car park – the Pay And Display on Jubilee Street,
the same chippy – chips with mushy peas on a tray and
  a can of Coke,
the same programme seller on the corner of Bullens Avenue
and always arriving an hour before kick off . . .
soaking up the atmosphere,
watching the players warm up
from the same seats – 267 and 268, just by the halfway line
with the same faces around us –

Big John red face

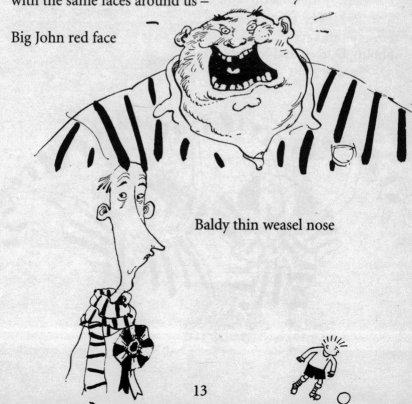

Baldy thin weasel nose

Bearded Bill the tattooed biker

Shouty Doreen and Mad Maureen

Pipe Smoke Bloke

And Old Man 'It wasn't like that in the old days'

But I love it.
Same time, same place,
Every home game
Always the same.

WEREWOLF DAD

Werewolf dad,
it's not a full moon once a month
but a home match every two weeks

he gradually changes,
once inside the ground he fidgets and twitches,
dribbles on his scarf and pie

just before kick-off
the veins on his neck stand out
and he bounces up and down on the spot

it's three o'clock and the change is complete,
the whistle blows and that's it . . .
howling and barking at the men in the middle

mild-mannered dad
to mad werewolf football fan
in ninety minutes plus injury time

POST-MATCH RITUALS

Going through the match afterwards with Dad,
almost kick by kick.

The what ifs, the nearly goals,
the almost theres and the
how things might have been different.

Savouring the glorious flavours of victory
or searching for the something sweet
among the bitter taste of defeat.

Either way the rituals are the same.
Going through the match afterwards with Dad,
almost kick by kick by kick . . .
by kick by kick . . . by kick . . .

ELEVENS

Poems that use eleven words only and reflect football team formations.

1 If we stand on the line perhaps they won't score

2 somehow

I don't think
our
formation
is balanced

enough to
work

3 we

all get   on   well

in   our   team except

for

him

4

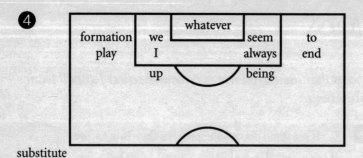

> formation play · we · I · whatever · seem · always · to · end · up · being · substitute

5

> our manager · have a · clue · what · doesn't · about · system · to · play

6

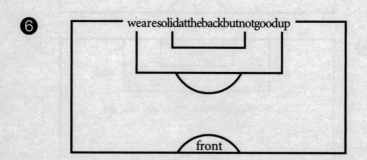

> wearesolidatthebackbutnotgoodup · front

7

last
week our manager tried to
play our five substitutes as well
but we still lost

8

their
centre   forward's
big   and
muscly   but
we're   not
scared   (honest)

9

every
shot we had
was off
nowhere near
the
goal   target

21

10

we

forget what system
we should play and
follow the ball
around

11

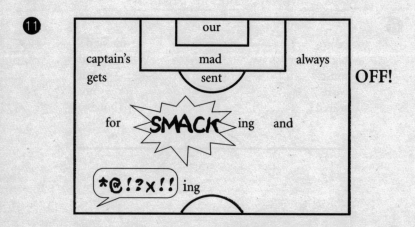

our

captain's   mad   always

gets   sent   **OFF!**

for   **SMACK**ing   and

✱@!?✗!! ing

introducing some of the team

DAVE TANKA

Built like a rhino
Lumbering and cumbersome
But dependable
Solid, no quarter given
Always scores his penalties

JAMIE CLERIHEW

Midfield dynamo, never thwarted
Plays for the team he's always supported
Always true blue through and through
Our very own Jamie Clerihew

WAYNE HAIKU (HAIKOONEY)

Seventeen years old
Already a shooting star
We wish and dream on

THIERRY CINQUAIN

Classy
Delicate touch
An artist with the ball
Threads passes through a needle's eye
God-like

BIG LEE MERICK

A tower of strength in each game
A powerful gigantic frame
Mean, moody, colossal
Of menace and muscle
A triumph of brawn over brain

TOMMY COUPLETSEN

Shining pate a-gleaming, mad eye crazy stare
Gritted teeth, determined, concentrated glare

Like a pirate on the seas ready for the plunder
Swashbuckling defences, tearing them asunder

Sharp and swift, decisive, committed to the cause
Mad Marauding Tommy deserving our applause

WATCHING THE MATCH ON TELETEXT

There may have been thrills
There may have been skills
Spills to make us nervous wrecks
But I wouldn't know
I couldn't go
I watched the match on teletext

There could have been passion
Goal mouth action
Chances spurned in front of nets
But how would I know
I couldn't go
I watched the match on teletext

A crowd of one on a front room night
TV on – black and white
Nil nil it says that's all right
What we might expect
Press the key, page three oh three
Mute the sound, no comment'ry
Then they've scored a penalty
One nil down on teletext

Scroll the pages, read the news
Other matches, other views
Praying we aren't going to lose
With once a minute checks
But every time the page comes on
Another minute's come and gone
We're still nil and they're still one
See the facts on teletext

Staring at the TV set
Hoping that it's incorrect
Anything could happen yet
And something great is next . . .
But full time comes and full time goes
That's two we've lost now in a row
And how we played I just don't know
I watched the match on teletext

POETRY IN MOTION

Scorer, striker, artist entertainer
Special skill standard maintainer
Never boring or mundaner
Highest quality campaigner

Turns on a sixpence
Predatory instincts
Measures any distance
In an instant

Lithe and lean – very acrobatical
A brain for the angles – very mathematical
Regal, royal – aristocratical
Theatrical – very dramatical
Standing ovations – the fans are fanatical

Show me a pair of heels that are cleaner
Or a physique that is leaner
Or a hunger that is keener
Or a finishing touch that's meaner
The grace and poise of a ballerina

Brain of a thinker, balance of a dancer
Ask him a question he's always got an answer
Every opportunity, every half chancer
Can he snap it up – of course he can sir . . .

The jinks, the dinks, the dribbles and tricks
The deft backheels and the delicate flicks
The punishing power, the bicycle kicks
The perfect placement slickety slick

GOAL!

Through defences, ghostly and haunting
Always dangerous, always daunting
Skill and ability, flair he's flaunting
Easing, teasing, testing and taunting

Pulling all the strings like a classical musician
Knows every trick just like a magician
Makes you feel better like a good physician
Feel the zeal of a man with a mission
Genius in any position
And he's a star you can wish-on

He's got a vision, clear and specific
Cold and clinical – very scientific
Takes every chance no matter how diffic-
Ult it is
The same res-
Ult it is

Man of the match – plays like a dream
We just wish he could play for our team.

HAIKUS

The crowd is full of
Fat men in replica shirts
Wishing they were stars

Shouting loud advice
On how to play the game when
They can't play themselves

COOLSCORIN' MATCHWINNIN' CELEBRATIN' STRIKER!

He's a shirt removin' crowd salutin'
handstandin' happy landin'
rockin' rollin' divin' slidin'
posin' poutin' loud shoutin'
pistol packin' smoke blowin'
flag wavin' kiss throwin'
hipswingin' armwavin'
breakdancin' cool ravin'
shoulder shruggin' team huggin'
hot shootin' rootin' tootin'
somersaultin' fence vaultin'
last minute goal grinnin'
shimmy shootin' shin spinnin'
celebratin' goalscorin' STRIKER!

MY GRANNY COULD SCORE THAT...

It was easier to score
Couldn't hit a barn door
What was he aiming for?
What on earth's he playing at?
One on one at last he's through
What on earth's he trying to do?
Missed it by a mile or two
My granny could score that!
And so could next door's cat!

How d'you miss an open goal?
He had time to take a stroll
Do you call that ball control?
What on earth's he playing at?
How much are we paying him?
Anyone could knock it in
Does he really want to win?
My granny could score that!
And so could next door's cat!

My granny's got a Zimmer frame
But she'd play better in this game
She has glasses but she'd aim to get it in the net no sweat
Next door's cat is old and past it
Always dozing in his basket
Even he could try and blast it in an open net, you bet.

It was easier to score
Couldn't hit a barn door
Missed a sitter once more
He needs looking at
If he can't see straight when he shoots
It's time to use the substitutes
They've both got their shooting boots
Granny and the cat,
They can't do worse than that!

My granny could score that!
And so could next door's cat!

if i WAS tHe ENGlAND MANAGeR

All opposition teams must wear pink.
And play in fluffy teddy bear slippers and tutus.

Their goalposts must be twenty feet high
and thirty-five feet wide
while ours can be reduced and moved
at a touch of a remote-controlled button
in my tracksuit pocket.

Matches will finish when I decide it is appropriate,
but only when we have scored more goals and are winning.
So games could last for three hours, a week, a month
or the full-time whistle may be blown
after two minutes if we get an early break-through.

Floodlights can be angled and altered in such a way
so that opposing goalkeepers are dazzled on high crosses.
Should that not work they can then be switched on and off
continuously until the desired effect is achieved.

In hot and humid matches
we are allowed to wear as much suntan cream as we want,
drink as much water and isotonic fluid as we want
and have a rest whenever we want.
The opposition, however, can only use cooking oil and
    Deep Heat
and must drink salt water and hot curried vegetable soup.

In cold and freezing conditions
we will wear our woolly gloves and hats,
thermal underwear and centrally heated shorts
but they must play in their pants and vests.
Or skins.

When we have a free kick defensive walls can stand within ten
    yards
although players are not allowed to protect themselves with
    their hands.

We must receive at least one penalty per game
while opposing goalkeepers are only allowed oven gloves
and a pair of horse's blinkers.

Our goalies meanwhile can utilize radar to detect dangerous
    crosses
and the liberal application of superglue.

World Cups will be ours,
the European Championships will be a formality
and record books will be rewritten forever
when I am the England Manager.

PROUD ENOUGH TO BURST

When I scored my first goal
for the school team
I felt so proud inside
that I thought it would bubble up
and I would burst
even though we lost five one.

A. C. ROSTIC - GOALKEEPER

Gargantuan, colossus, somewhat god-like
Omnipresent guardian of the goals
A giant among mortals, superhuman
Lord of the area he patrols
Keeper of the nets, he keeps them empty
Everything he touches he controls
Even shots of thunder and deflections
Perfect timing, joyous to behold
Ever the invincible of athletes
Reflexes of lightning, touch of gold

twenty things NEEDED FOR A GAME
of FOOTBALL in the LOCAL PARK

1. Even number of players with at least four wearing anoraks or duffel coats.

2. Remove anoraks or duffel coats to use as goalposts.

3. Pick teams

4. Do not pick smallest or fattest ones last.

5. Get out ball.

6. Argue with each other as to whose turn it was to bring ball.

7. Borrow friend's bike to go home and fetch ball.

8. Meanwhile, practise the art of spitting and clearing the nose.

9. Get out ball.

10. Argue with person who brought the ball as to why it is flat.

11. Borrow another friend's bike to fetch pump and adaptor.

12. Meanwhile practise rude words to shout at non-existent referee.

13. Pump up ball.

14. Kick off and start game.

15. Commentate like John Motson on passing movements and eventual shot.

16. Argue whether shot
    a) missed
    b) went in
    c) went over the anorak post
    d) would have hit post and either gone in or bounced out.

17. Try to retrieve ball from muddy ditch behind goals.

18. Do not head ball for at least fifteen minutes.

19. Get jeans as dirty as possible because the dirtier they are the better you must have played.

20. Play until
    a) everyone goes home
    b) it is too dark to see
    c) you are winning
    d) you are winning, it is too dark to see and it is your ball anyway so you're going home anyway so there.

PERFECT

Perfect.
Innocuous at first,
the ball looping over,
no real danger, nothing much on.

But he saw it first,
acting instinctively and swiftly,
stretching every single muscle
to claim first touch, the decisive kick.

Couldn't have been placed better . . .
the unreachable arc of the ball
spinning above the stranded guardian
in slow, slow, s l o o o w w w motion.

The billow of the net from the kiss of the ball
Perfect.
Well it would have been
if it had been at the other end of the pitch.

tHE FUtURE'S BRiGHt

He's star of the future,
coming through the ranks,
only sixteen.

World class stamped all over,
a future England regular,
a name for the record books.

Not only is he in our team
But our fans have seen him first
and already taken him to their hearts.

Already, his name is on their terraced lips.

Already, there are chants for the chance
to see a hero in the making.

Already, there are roars and applause
for the goals this legend in progress scores.

Patience is difficult when stardom strongly beckons
but we have seen the prophecy,
we have seen what is to come.

We have seen the future
and the future is bright,
the future is blue.

HALF-TiME

PIE QUEUE

Sometimes the only

Thing to look forward to is

The pie at half-time

ACROSTIC HALF-TIME

After forty-five minutes of Hurried, yet passionate football havE
Come and gone with wave After wave of pressure from our teaM
Resulting in no goals so far Let's hope they can just carry on and I
Only have more to cheer on aFter the half-time team talk and resT

So, here's hoping our team geT the early pressure and score the goaL
That will give us the self confIdence to play the ball about with skilL
Incredible ease and score a nuMber of fantastic goals so me and yoU
Can cheer the victory with gleE thus forgetting the goalless first halF

Mid-Season Poem

Not so bad at all,
Better than we could have hoped for.

Fifth in the Premiership,
Lost only two in the last twelve.

The revelation of the youngster
And the class of the new signing.

The speed and feet of fire of our striker
And the bite of the midfield general.

The spirit and the confidence,
The leadership of the manager.

Hardworking without sparkling,
Challenging without shining.

At this rate we'll be safe by January,
No relegation worries come May.

Nosebleeds, ladders and vertigo,
We're getting used to dizzy heights.

So far, so good,
Here's to the future, it's only just begun.

SECOND HALF

MY UNCLE PERCY ONCE REMOVED

My Uncle Percy once removed
his bobble hat, scarf, overcoat,
woolly jumper, string vest,
flared trousers and purple Y-fronts
and ran on to the pitch at Wembley
during a Cup Final
and was at once removed
by six stewards and nine officers of the law.
Once they'd caught him.

PENALTIES

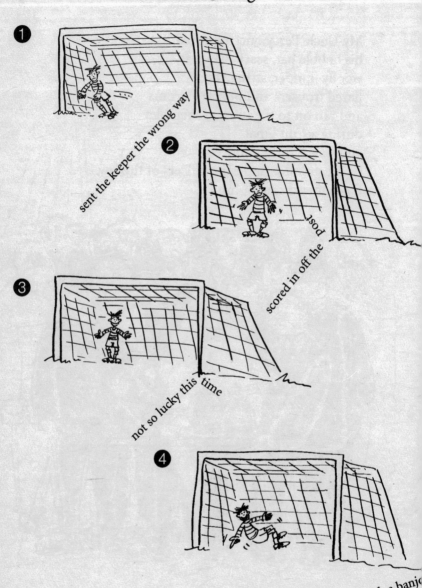

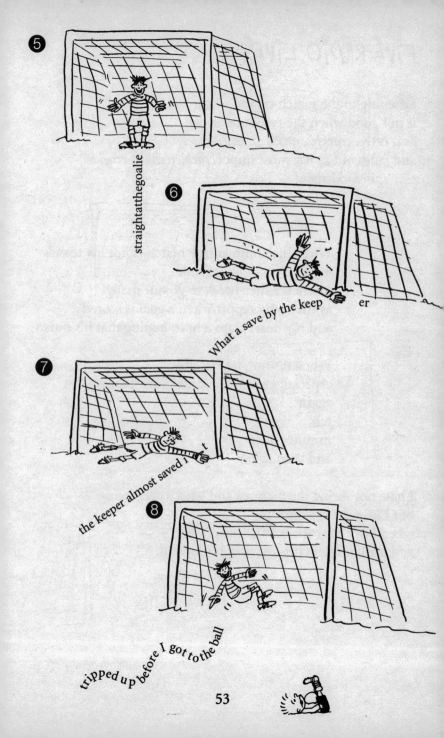

5

straight at the goalie

6

What a save by the keeper

7

the keeper almost saved it

8

tripped up before I got to the ball

53

FIVE RADIO LIVES

Listening to the match on the radio
is not good when the reception is bad
as it often *cracklescracklesfizzzzcrackles*
and fades out at *fizz* most impor*cracklefizz*tant *crackle*
mo*crackle*ment

When the commentary match is not my team's
my heart is in my mouth
whenever they break to go our match
as they only report when a goal is scored
and my heart skips a beat, hoping that it's ours.

When it's not, it's horrible,
especially when the same thing happens
again
ten
minutes later
and then again.

I hate not seeing the pictures and what's happening
but I love the excitement
when I can hear the roar of the crowd
and the commentators go absolutely wild.

Sometimes I get so mad when we are losing
that I switch off in anger and stomp about
only to switch it back on again
straight away
just in case things have changed.

A goal is a goal is a goal.
Even when I'm alone in my room
with only a radio
a goal is a goal is a goal
and always something to celebrate.

MR KENNING — THE REFEREE

Match starter
Watch watcher
Time keeper
Play stopper

Decision maker
Foul ignorer
Blind eye-er
Game changer

Headline causer
Finger pointer
Penalty giver
Card waver

Crowd incensor
Hassle taker
Abuse listener
No mate-er

Hot seater
Black wearer
Gun sticker
Whistle blower

WOW!

First Half . . .

The atmosphere's electric at
The all engrossing action packed
All absorbing captivating rip roaring fascinating
Heady and intoxicating fever pitch exhilarating
Pulse quickening adrenaline pumping
Senses reeling heartbeat thumping
End to end and inspired
Rock and roller coaster ride

Second Half . . .

It's a topsy turvy give and take
Hundred mile an hour rate
Spell binding hypnotic
Kamikaze chaotic
Thrills, spills, incident filled
Special and sensational
Enthralling inspirational
Nerve shredding mind blowing
Total draining never slowing
Enthusiastic most fantastic football match you've ever been at
You can't take your eyes of the action for a minute
Never has ninety minutes had so much packed in it.

Full time.

I'm a blaster not a tapper
A ninety-minute scrapper
A chopper and a hacker
No one passes me

I've got the brawn and muscle
For the tackle and the tussle
I will hassle and I'll hustle
No one passes me

Harum-scarum do or dare 'em
I will take the knocks and bare 'em
Show me strikers and I'll scare
Any team and I will stir 'em

I'm a winner not a loser
A rough 'em touch 'em bruiser
A goal scorer's confuser
No one passes me

Summer sun or winter mire
Lion hearted do a die-er
In my belly burns a fire
I'm the one who can inspire

I'm a last-ditch tackle fighter
A knee and ankle bighter
Nobody marks you tighter
Cos no one passes me

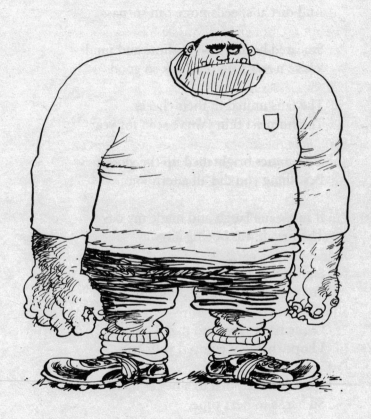

DEAR REFEREE

I saw you when you fell and slipped
Upon the greasy mud and tripped

You slid headfirst along the grass
And dirt at speeds none can surpass

Smeared head to toe in slime and mud
We've never seen refs look so good

The fans united in their cheers
The funniest thing we've seen for years

Your antics brightened up the gloom
Best thing you did all afternoon

It made me laugh and made my day
The match was boring anyway.

Signed and meant, sincerely yours
For once deserving of applause.

Come back soon and may I quip
I hope that you enjoyed your trip.

It couldn't happen to a better man
So here's to next time,
                              A football fan

GRATE

Saturday afternoon, three o'clock
and I wish I wasn't here.
I'm daydreaming about the match . . .
the sound of the crowd, the thwack of the ball
and my usual seat . . .

Instead I'm sitting upright in an old Victorian armchair
in a dusty, old-fashioned front room
listening to Mum's Great-aunt Alice
going on and on and on about the price of bread
and dead relatives I've never heard of.

Ten to five.
We're still here
and I've had a cup of strong tea in a china cup
and half of one of her rock cakes
(that actually taste like they have real rocks in),
I've been told that children should be seen and not heard
and I'm trying to imagine the match . . .
what's the score, are we winning,
have we played better than last week?

Great-aunt Alice hates football,
won't turn the telly on for the results
so I've got to wait till later,
the tension's unbearable
and while I do hope that we won
and won convincingly
part of me hopes that I haven't missed
the best match of the season so far,
a truly great match.

That would grate,
just like being here with Great-aunt Alice.

JuSt One Of tHOSe GAMeS

Every little touch and trick was magic
Everything he touched just turned to dust
Every single pass reached its target
Ballooning passes straight up into touch
Every tackle total and well-timed
Tackles later than a much-delayed train
Every fifty-fifty ball was his
Slipped and fell then slipped and fell again
Quick-thinking, speedy, fleet of foot
Cumbersome and seemed to wade in honey
Right place, right time, right direction
Wrong, wrong, wrong but always funny
Majestic in the air for every high ball
Concussed and banged his goalie on the head
Every shot he had went on target
Either his own players or Row Zed
Almost telepathic with his team mates
Couldn't find his own team with a map
Timed his runs to absolute perfection
Always caught out by the offside trap
Scored a hat trick of the highest calibre
Couldn't hit a barn door with a banjo
Hit the woodwork twice and won a penalty

To cap it all he scored a great own goal
Everything just worked, he didn't put a foot wrong
Nothing could be worse, couldn't do a thing right
On top of his game and really on song
He couldn't have changed if he'd played all night
Dazzling, brilliant, a blinder, on fire
A stinker, a horror, a nightmare that's rotten
A match to be remembered forever
A match to be forgotten!

Everybody's different, no one is the same
Good or bad, just one of those games.

MAN OF THE MATCH?!

The telly made him man of the match,
scorer of two goals that won the match.
Not just any old match
but the EUFA Cup Final.

He wasn't my man of the match though . . .
He'd been stretchered off three times
from non-descript tackles that left him rolling . . .
and diving and screaming and shouting
as if he'd been poleaxed by a sharp shooting sniper
only to recover a few seconds later
and go galloping gazelle-like round the pitch once again.

Actor of the match – maybe.
Certainly not *man* though.
Big-girl's-blouse-softy-kid-pretending-to-be-hurt-of-the-
    match.
Definitely.

tHE BEST BiT ABOUt tHE MATCH

It wasn't the fact that we won
– well, it was because we came back from 1–0 down and
   won 4–1.
but it was made better by the fact
that when they scored their first goal
their centre forward celebrated by removing his shirt
and waving it helicopter-like around his head
sprinted towards the away fans.

That would have been fine
except that before he got there
the shirt flew out of his hands
and flew into the home fans,
where it stayed for the next three and a half minutes.

And when it was thrown back
it only had one arm.

MAGIC AND LOSS

The magic of the FA Cup
The giant killing dream
Everyone wants an upset but
Not against their team

The romance of the fight
The tie that steals the scene
Everyone wants an upset but
Not against their team

The struggle and the glory
The drama of the story
It's all on ninety minutes
A bit of luck could win it
Eleven v. eleven
Dreams of cup tie heaven
It's a level field of play
It's all about the day

The magic of the FA Cup
The giant killing dream
Everyone wants an upset but
Not against their team

tHiNGS CouLD HAVE BEEN DiffERENt

Things could have been different.
No, really.
They could.

At one all, all square,
everything to play for
and three missed chances,
two of them easier to score ones to boot.

A free kick and a soft penalty
– both never should have been
and then we lose.

True, I'm ignoring certain things . . .
the five class saves our keeper made
and two shots against the woodwork.

But three missed chances,
just think how it might have been different,
very different.

Yes,
we could have lost 9–4
instead of just 2–1.

FOOTBALL CHANTS THAT DIDN'T CATCH ON

> Who's the nice man in the black?
> We all love the referee!
> His eyesight's always perfect!
> Yes we all agree – ee!

Offside! Never mind!
2 – 4 – 6 – 8! The other team is really great!
Yes it was a very good goal
Even though it was against us!

> Ooh we like the colours on your shirts!
> We lost but you played well!
> We shared all the pies!
> Nil nil! Nil nil! Nil nil! Nil nil!

See you at the next match then!
Ooh ah ooh ah! Oh what sporting fans you are!
Wemberlee! Wemberlee! It used to be a stadium
    and they called it Wemberlee!
And you'll never walk alone – especially when our
    coach can give you a lift home!

FORTUNE FAVOURS tHE BRAVE

Fortune favours the brave
A smash and grab goal and penalty save
A brilliant stop and the crowd forgave
This week's hero, last week's knave
It may have been a close close shave
Thanks to the woodwork we can crave
All three points and shout and wave
We can chant and we can rave
Fortune favours the brave.

LOOKING FOR SIGNS OF HOPE
AMONGST THE WRECKAGE OF DEFEAT

Even though we lost
I still want to see the highlights on the telly,
not to relive the pain of loss
but to search for signs of hope,
scan for signs of anything remotely positive:
those moments on which a match might turn.
I want to see the shots that went agonizingly wide,
the chances carelessly spurned,
the hard work, endeavour and commitment,
the touches of skill – should there be any.

I want to see the mistakes that led to the goals against,
the referee's decisions that changed the game –
giving advantage where it wasn't deserved,
the free kicks we didn't get
and the rebounds that just didn't quite fall.

I want to scrutinize these for signs of hope,
those moments on which a match might turn
and pretend that in some small way
we will learn from them
so that not only do they not happen again
but also that there might be a game
where everything goes to plan
and the variables combine to perfection,
the shots go in,
the chances are snapped up,
the decisions go in our favour,
rebounds fall kindly
so that one day we may have that day
when things are different.

I have that dream.

tHAt SinKiNG FEELiNG

It's that sinking feeling
in the pit of your stomach,
the lump in the throat,
that numbness and the nothingness
when you've watched your favourite football team
lose.
They had the chances but couldn't score.
They gave away an easy goal.
They didn't play as well as they did in the last match.

It's that sinking feeling
when you feel like shutting yourself away
until all your best friends forget the score.
Buy they never do
and they take every opportunity
to remind you in great and fondest detail
with their slow motion replay commentary.

It's that sinking feeling
when despite the last fifteen minutes of pressure,
near misses, goalmouth scrambles and amazing saves
they just weren't good enough on the day
and no matter what you say or do
the score remains the same.

It's that sinking feeling
when the most you can hope for
is that your best friend's favourite team
lost by more goals than yours.

THE FOOTBALL RESULTS ARE AS FOLLOWS

The game was	1	derful hope you enjoyed it	2
I don't know if	5	ever seen a better match be	4
Now I'm feelin	0	not just because of the pie I	8
Scoring that many's	7	but hell for them because we	1
At last we reached our po	10	tial with our talented first	11
All their supporters are	6	as parrots they just couldn't go	1
Playing with total	3	dom we will always domin	8
It was our vir	2	uoso performance they just couldn't sur	5

DREAMS OF EUROPE

Dreams of Europe shining bright
Riding high, top flight
End of season in sight
Dreams of Europe shining bright

Dreams of Europe fade away
Lost another match today
Three points needed, one to play
Dreams of Europe fade away

Dreams of Europe torn and tattered
Couldn't win when it mattered
Fans are feeling down and shattered
Dreams of Europe torn and tattered

Dreams of Europe dead and gone
Dreams of Europe carry on
Dreams of Europe
Dreams . . .

tHE WEATHER, tHE WiNNiNG AND tHE LOSiNG

On those days when we win
the bad weather doesn't matter one bit
but on those days when we don't
every raindrop pummels home the defeat,
every ice blast of wind chills the weary bones,
every snowflake in the eyes freezes frustration's tears
and the longing for home and a hot drink increases
  infinitely.

The cold feels colder
the wet feels wetter
everything's worse
nothing's better
but on the days that we win
nothing else matters.

GOAL OF THE SEASON

Unstoppable – a belter
A real goal-net melter

Unreachable – a stinger
A sizzling humdinger

Umsaveable – a blaster
A hundred mile right past you

Untouchable – a screamer
A centre forward dream-er

Unforgettable – a scorcher
A form of goalie torture

Unrepeatable – a winner
A never quite the same again-er

Unique – the reason
The goal of the season

POEM FOR THE LAST DAY OF THE FOOTBALL SEASON

It looked so good
Halfway through
Unfulfilled
Potential blue

Early exits
From each cup
Safe and sound
But not quite up

We could have done
So much more
Lost too many
Couldn't score

Signs of hope
With good reason
Same time same place
Next football season

EXTRA tiME

Savour the Flavour – the Taste of Success

Savour the flavour – the taste of success
The sinning, the grinning when we are the best
The smiles last for miles outshining the rest
We savour the flavour – the taste of success

The joy in the joining of sweet celebration
The victory chants, the songs of elation
Losing ourselves in complete celebration
The joy in the joining of sweet celebration

We're winners, we're victors, we've beaten the rest
The FA Cup Final, the best of the best
Flying our colours we've passed every test
We savour the flavour – the taste of success.

ALL THAT MATTERED

ENGLAND 1 ARGENTINA 0

It wasn't the best penalty in the world
but that didn't matter.
It wasn't the best penalty in the World Cup
but that didn't matter.
It may not have even been a penalty
but that didn't matter either.

What did matter
was that it was our penalty
and that it was our penalty
against Argentina.

It wasn't the best-taken penalty ever
but that didn't matter.
Straight down the middle of the goal
but that didn't matter.
If the goalie had stood still he would have saved it
but that didn't matter either.

What did matter
was that Beckham took it,
wanted to take it
blasted it
made no mistake
and scored
1–0.
That's all that mattered.

GERMANY 1 ENGLAND 5

Once every so often it happens
It feels like it's never going to happen
and sometimes it doesn't
but once every so often it actually happens.

Once every so often
you see a football match so special
that it becomes part of the national heritage,
a match that takes on legendary status,
folklore and glory.

Dads and grandads have had their 1966 . . .
Hurst, Moore, Peters, Charlton, Ball et al
England 4 West Germany 2.

Big brothers and uncles had 1996,
trouncing Holland 4–1.

But what have we had?
Lost penalty shoot outs, early exits
and never quite reaching any potential.

Until now . . .

We watched it, couldn't quite believe our eyes,
but we watched it, smiling, cheering, laughing, revelling
and we were part of the shared experience
of history in the making
when fate conspires
to juggle all the variables in our favour
so that even when going 1–0 down
every chance is taken and we get to demolish Germany,
yes . . . demolish Germany 5–1.

To score five is remarkable.
To score five away from home is amazing.
To score five away from home against Germany
is not just remarkable and amazing but almost unreal.

Owen – three, a hat trick,
Gerrard and Heskey, one apiece.
History, real history
and even while the teams still played
we knew then that this was the match we had been waiting
   for for so long,
that this match was indeed history in the making,
a match to remember.

Our match to remember.

TONIGHT I PLAYED LIKE BECKHAM, TODAY HE PLAYED LIKE ME

ENGLAND 2: GREECE 2

Tonight I played like Beckham,
today he played like me.
True, I haven't got the skill
and I can't bend it like him.
OK, I didn't score the free kick against Greece
that took us to the World Cup
– mine went over the hedge and into next door's
  greenhouse –
but tonight I played like Beckham
and today he played like me.

It wasn't anything to do with ability
but everything to do with attitude.
He was like the kid on the park,
anoraks for goalposts,
wanting to kick every single ball,
be involved in every single move,
tackle every single tackle.
His position went out of the window,
he was everywhere
left, right, centre, attack and defence,
like a bee around the honey pot.

And it was because of that,
because he was once again that kid on the park
who'll play till it's dark
that kid who'll carry on
because he doesn't want to lose
that tonight I played a little bit like Beckham
and today he played a little bit like me.

Except he was better.

APPENDIX

For those interested, some of the poems were based on real people and real matches. They are:

The Future's Bright: there's only one Wayne Rooney!

Watching the Match on Teletext: Southampton 1 Everton 0

Dave Tanka – David Unsworth (sort of!)

Tommy Coupletsen – Thomas Gravesen

Wayne Haiku – Wayne Rooney

Big Lee Merick – Big Duncan Ferguson

Poetry in Motion: I suppose I had someone like Thierry Henry in mind

Perfect: Alan Stubbs' own goal against Fulham. Sorry Stubbsy!

Mid-Season Poem: that's how it was!

The Defender You Depend on: Alan Stubbs springs to mind here . . .

Magic And Loss: Shrewsbury Town 2 Everton 1 – nuff said

Things Could Have Been Different: Everton 1 Manchester United 2

Goal of the Season: Either Wayne Rooney's winner against Arsenal or Tomasz Radzinski's winner against Southampton. Both of them are belters!

Dreams of Europe: last few matches of the season . . .

Fortune Favours the Brave: Richard Wright's penalty save against Sunderland.

Savour the Flavour: Everton 1 Manchester United 0 – 1995 FA Cup Final

Man of the Match – whoever was Man of the Match in the 2003 EUFA Final

The 'Extra Time' matches are self explanatory